Clubs and Resorts

DESIGNING FOR RECREATION AND LEISURE

Clubs and Resorts
DESIGNING FOR RECREATION AND LEISURE

Architecture & Interior Design Library

An Imprint of
PBC INTERNATIONAL, INC.

Distributor to the trade in the United States and Canada
Rizzoli International Publications Inc.
300 Park Avenue South
New York, NY 10010

Distributor to the art trade in the United States and Canada
PBC International, Inc.
One School Street
Glen Cove, NY 11542
1-800-527-2826
Fax 516-676-2738

Distributor throughout the rest of the world
Hearst Books International
1350 Avenue of the Americas
New York, NY 10019

Library Of Congress Cataloging–in–Publication Data

Clubs and resorts / by the editors of PBC International, Inc.
    p. cm.
    Includes index.
    ISBN 0–86636–230–4   international version 0-86636-293-2
    1. Architecture and recreation. 2. Resort architecture. I. PBC International.
NA2543.R43C58 1994   93–30033
725' .8--dc20   CIP

CAVEAT– Information in this text is believed accurate, and will pose no problem for the stu-
dent or casual reader. However, the author was often constrained by information contained in
signed release forms, information that could have been in error or not included at all. Any mis-
information (or lack of information) is the result of failure in these attestations. The author has
done whatever is possible to insure accuracy.

Color separation, printing and binding by
C & C Offset Printing Co., Ltd.

Printed in Hong Kong

10 9 8 7 6 5 4 3 2 1

INTRODUCTION

Today's hectic lifestyle and stressful conditions create a need for leisure spots. No longer the hideaways of the rich and famous, these various clubs, spas and resorts are the refuges from the pressures and tribulations of everyday life; they are an escape, an oasis.

This book contains over 45 international projects that showcase outstanding leisure spots— from a breathtaking golf club in Tokyo; to the Canyon Ranch Spa in Lenox, Massachusetts; to a fishing lodge in California; to a beach resort in the Fiji Islands; to a multi-level health and recreation complex in New York. Each of these getaways provides a respite, a haven to refresh one's mind, one's body and one's spirit.

Sit back, relax, and take a journey around the world to some of the leading spas and resorts.

I
PART

Clubs

■

The Falls Club
Blackhawk, California

PROJECT TYPE:
Country Club

DESIGN TEAM:
Steve Chase, Cheri Kelley, Doug Dahlin

ARCHITECTURAL/DESIGN FIRM:
Steve Chase Associates Interior Design;
The Dahlin Group (architects)

PROJECT SIZE:
15,000 square feet

PHOTOGRAPHY:
© 1991 Steve Whittaker

A cross between the colors and materials native to California and those that reflect the contemporary "style" of the state is exhibited in the Falls Club, located in Blackhawk, California. The club is kept in balance with its surroundings through the use of such materials as native stone in the flooring, tables, light, and natural wood finishes in the walls and ceilings. The curved glass wall that encircles the restaurant affords views of a waterway formed from natural stone. Pastel colors in mauve and turquoise warm the large space and give it a "California" feel. The large Coromandel screen, a major piece of art fortunately left over from another project—the club's budget would never have allowed its purchase—serves as the focal point for the dining room area.

The Blackhawk Club is meant to be more of a golf club than a social club.

Nevertheless, in one large building it offers both bar and dining rooms, a commercial kitchen, lounge, and full pro shop. Overall, the harmonious look achieved is a perfect balance between the traditional and the natural for this young and growing country club.

Sunhills Country Club
Tokyo, Japan

PROJECT TYPE:
Country Club

DESIGN TEAM:
Michael James Leineweber, AIA, Vice Chairman (Project Director); Bon-Hui Uy, Director of Design (Designer); R. Ted Matheny, Project Manager; Lorrie Dalton, Senior Vice President (Senior Interior Designer)

ARCHITECTURAL/DESIGN FIRM:
Media Five Limited

PROJECT SIZE:
80,000 square feet

BUDGET:
$20 million

PHOTOGRAPHY:
Kawasumi Architectural Photograph Office

Providing visitors with the ultimate in resort facilities and amenities, Tokyo's Sunhills Country Club features east and west golf courses designed by world-renowned Robert Trent Jones II that qualify as international championship courses. The club projects a contemporary look, with the clubhouse and hotel designed in a modified "L" shape connected by a projected half-circular form to command a full view of the golf course. The spa and baths are accessed from the main level through marble-trimmed doorways. In both men's and women's facilities, a corridor with sculpted ceiling leads to dressing rooms, lockers, Japanese-style

bathing areas with seating ledges and furos fed by natural hot springs. The men's facilities also include a rotenburo (outdoor bath) and a VIP lounge area.

The main dining room, competition rooms, VIP lounges and guest rooms are located on the second level. Large skylights and natural lighting play integral roles in the architectural design, while baffles and an articulated ceiling with decorative arches draw the eye up and toward the light. The 14-foot wide gallery corridor acts as a long pedestrian promenade, with inset carpeting in three tones to create a series of border patterns. The space is interrupted

by potted trees and seating arrangements of bleached teak "porch-style" benches and faux stone tables. To provide guests with the feeling of an exclusive resort, warm coral tones with tropical blue accents were selected to offset the cooler climate of Tochigi Prefecture.

A spectacular 180-degree view of the golf course interspersed with soft accent wall sconces provide further visual interest for the 130-seat restaurant. An entertainment lounge for cocktails, music and dancing is located on the club's third level. Outdoor facilities include a pool, tennis courts, and a heliport.

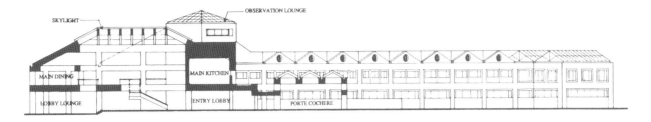

BUILDING SECTION 'A'

GRAPHIC SCALE   1:200

BUILDING SECTION 'B'

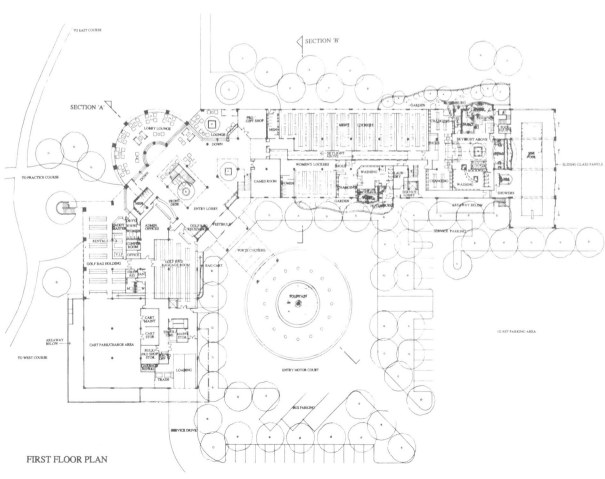

FIRST FLOOR PLAN

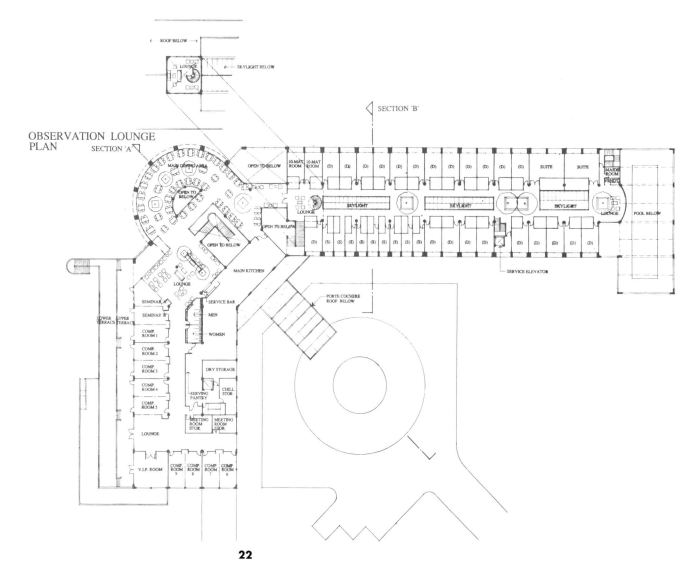

OBSERVATION LOUNGE
PLAN

SECTION 'A'

SECTION 'B'

ROOF BELOW

SKYLIGHT BELOW

LOUNGE

MAIN DINING AREA

OPEN TO BELOW

OPEN TO BELOW

OPEN TO BELOW

LOUNGE

SEMINAR A

SERVICE BAR

SEMINAR B

MEN

COMP. ROOM 1

WOMEN

COMP. ROOM 2

LOWER UPPER TERRACE TERRACE

COMP. ROOM 3

DRY STORAGE

COMP. ROOM 4

SERVING PANTRY

CHILL STOR.

COMP. ROOM 5

MEETING ROOM STOR.

MEETING ROOM STOR.

LOUNGE

V.I.P. ROOM

COMP ROOM 9

COMP ROOM 8

COMP ROOM 7

COMP ROOM 6

MAIN KITCHEN

PORTE COCHERE ROOF BELOW

10-MAT ROOM

10-MAT ROOM

LOUNGE

SKYLIGHT

SKYLIGHT

SKYLIGHT

SUITE

SUITE

MAIDS ROOM FENZO

LOUNGE

POOL BELOW

SERVICE ELEVATOR

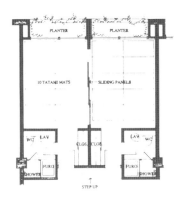

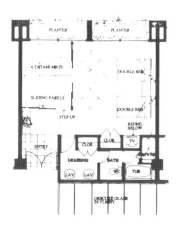

The South Caolina Yacht Club
Hilton Head Island, South Carolina

PROJECT TYPE:
Yacht Club/Marina

DESIGN TEAM:
Dottie Hawkins (Interior Design)

ARCHITECTURAL/DESIGN FIRM:
Chris Schmitt & Associates Inc. (Architectural design); Keane Robinson Architects (Contract Documents & Construction Administration); EPA (Landscape Architecture)

PROJECT SIZE:
13,000 square feet

BUDGET:
$1,500,000

PHOTOGRAPHY:
© Rion Rizzo / Creative Sources Photography

Intended to be the premier yachting center along the South Carolina coast, this multi-purpose club is the focal point of a 450 slip fresh-water marina. The marina, which uses a state-of-the art lock system to keep the water level at a constant 8-foot depth, accommodates yachts up to 70 feet in length. The club building's architectural style combines traditional nautical features such as the widow's walk and nautical flag pole with materials and detailing that reflect the architectural heritages of the nearby historic cities of Savannah and Charleston. Principal building materials include a green standing seam metal roof, yellow stucco walls with detailing in relief, treated wood decks, and white wood windows and trim.

Due to its location in the coastal flood zone, the club building had to be elevated a full story above the existing grade at the edge of the marina, so the space below the flood plain was utilized for storage and yachting activity functions. This added height, along with its central location in the marina gives the building, with its many decks, spectacular views of the marina and surrounding areas.

Traditional detailing and materials are continued in the interior of the yacht club, that features an 85 seat restaurant, a 50 seat bar/lounge, a library/trophy room, a meeting room that seats 100, a boardroom, and club offices. Flanking the central hall on the main level are the restaurant and the bar/lounge and library/trophy room. Upstairs, the hall is balanced on one side by the meeting room and on the other by the boardroom and offices.

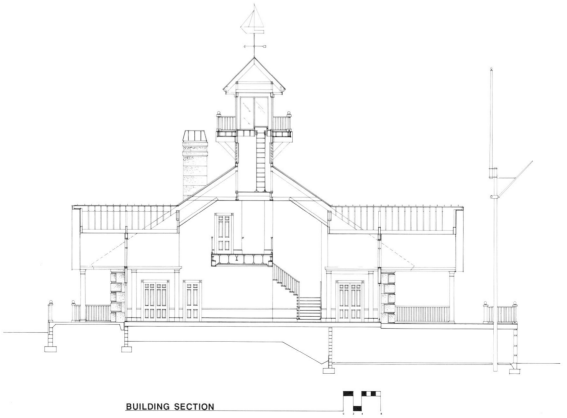

BUILDING SECTION

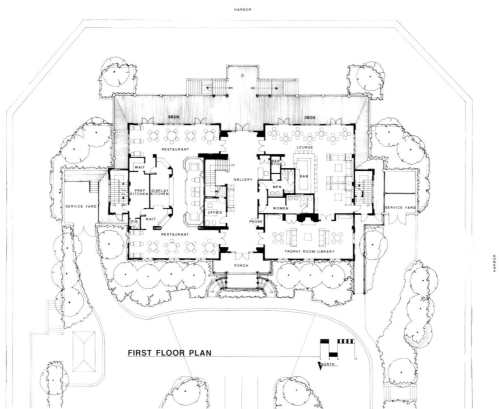

FIRST FLOOR PLAN

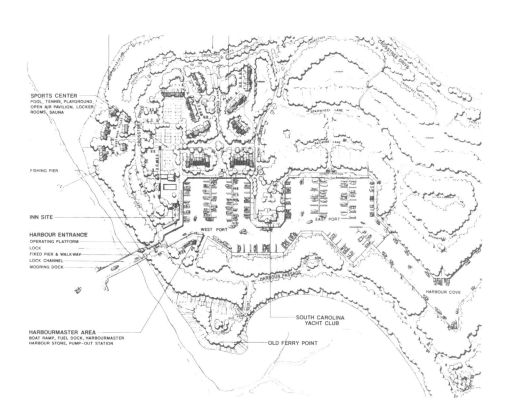

SPORTS CENTER
POOL, TENNIS, PLAYGROUND
OPEN AIR PAVILION, LOCKER
ROOMS, SAUNA

FISHING PIER

INN SITE

HARBOUR ENTRANCE
OPERATING PLATFORM
LOCK
FIXED PIER & WALKWAY
LOCK CHANNEL
MOORING DOCK

WEST PORT

EAST PORT

SOUTH CAROLINA
YACHT CLUB

HARBOUR PASSAGE

HARBOUR COVE

HARBOURMASTER AREA
BOAT RAMP, FUEL DOCK, HARBOURMASTER
HARBOUR STORE, PUMP-OUT STATION

OLD FERRY POINT

Mission Bay Golf Center
San Francisco, California

PROJECT TYPE:
Driving Range and Golf Learning Center

DESIGN TEAM:
Darryl Roberson, FAIA, Principal in charge; Jerry Griffin, AIA; Fred Quezada, AIA

ARCHITECTURAL/DESIGN FIRM:
STUDIOS Architecture,
Chris Patillo & Associates
(Landscape Architecture)

PROJECT SIZE:
two levels, 66 tees

BUDGET:
$2.2 million

PHOTOGRAPHY:
© Sharon Risedorph; image of many golfers on turret golf course by © Mike Joyce

The Mission Bay Golf Center is a driving range/teaching facility located on 9.25 acres in San Francisco's South of Market District, and the facility, the first on the West coast to be located downtown, is within minutes of major office buildings and hotels. The centerpiece of the development is a two-tier driving structure featuring 33 tees per level. The curving 330-foot exposed steel frame with suspended roof canopies overlooks a 330-yard-long landscaped fairway. Diaphanous fabric used throughout allows views back to the downtown skyline while protecting golfers from San Francisco's bone-chilling fog.

The design solution responds to the gritty urban context with an honest industrial aesthetic. A rationalist structural expression is consistently exposed in both steel and wood buildings. Eighty foot high perimeter netting poles are set in 30 foot deep driven hollow steel caissons. The cafe and pro shop are housed in utilitarian mobile modules which are visually enhanced with carefully detailed wood frame shade structures and decks. The colorful, inviting scale of a facility normally associated with suburban country clubs provides a pleasing atmosphere for urban recreation.

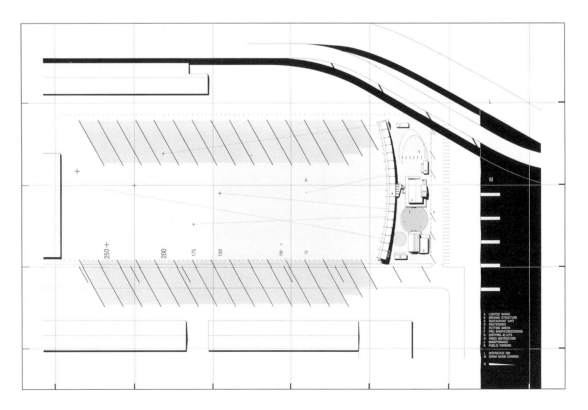

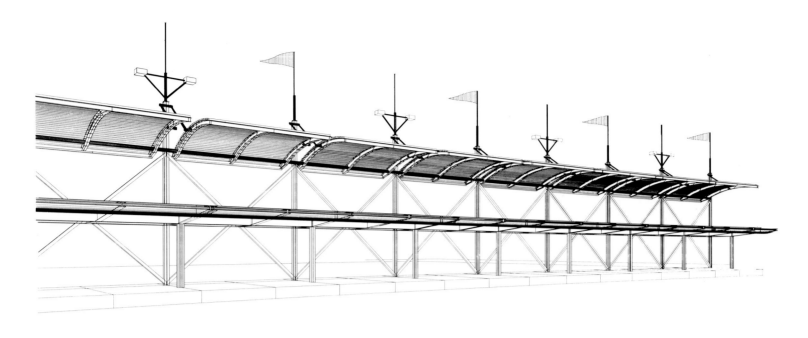

Palm Hills Golf Club House
Okinawa, Japan

PROJECT TYPE:
Golf Clubhouse

DESIGN TEAM:
John Grinnell, Senior Project Designer; Kathleen Sauter, Senior Decorator; J. Patrick Lawrence, AIA, Principal in Charge; Jon Pharis, AIA, Project Designer

ARCHITECTURAL/DESIGN FIRM:
Hirsch/Bedner Associates (interior design); Wimberly Allison Tong & Goo (architecture); Bau Architects & Associates

PROJECT SIZE:
135,000 square feet

PHOTOGRAPHY:
© Robert Miller

The Okinawa Palm Hills Golf Club House is an imposing statement of Mediterranean style, with large roof forms that create a residential scale. The dominant feature of the Palm Hills structure is a semicircular 70-foot-tall atrium, featuring a grand staircase that splays in two directions and a large expanse of glass that faces the Ronald Frame 18-hole golf course. Because the location is vulnerable to lightning storms and typhoons, the finial atop the atrium holds a lightning rod, one of three on the building's roof, and the areas surrounding the glass contain an anchorage system to which protective panels are attached during storms.

Guests enter through the Lobby Concourse and an arched gallery flanked by a "colonnade" of jet ceramic jardinieres. A Thomas McNight painting serves as a focal point for the custom reception desk. An overhead cut crystal chandelier and custom carpeting based on an indigenous Okinawan pattern add to the beauty of the space. On the main floor, an owner's suite includes an office, lounge, bar, terrace and Japanese-style bath. The lower level features a pro shop, terrace bar, locker rooms and private gardens. The Men's Bath, also on this level, combines a palatial rendition of Japanese bathing cus-

toms with Western innovations. Amenities include a furo or soaking bath surrounded by natural stone, a marble columned jacuzzi matched by a similar cold plunge, showers, scrub-down areas and a water massage wall. The entire bath enjoys a garden view, walled for privacy. The clubhouse also features several dining rooms, meeting rooms and bars, and an elaborately residential VIP Lounge with large and roomy seating and objets d'art from the owner's personal collection.

Wonderland Race Track
Revere, Massachusetts

PROJECT TYPE:
Greyhound Racetrack

DESIGN TEAM:
Morris Nathanson, President; Peter A. Niemitz; Vice-President; Blase Gallo, Project Captain, Vice-President of Design; Project Supervisor for client, Mark Hartzfeld

ARCHITECTURAL/DESIGN FIRM:
Morris Nathanson Design

BUDGET:
$5 million

PHOTOGRAPHY:
© Warren Jagger, Warren Jagger Photography, Inc.

*Billed as "the most sophisti-*cated greyhound track in the country," the new Wonderland Racetrack represents the complete redesign and modernization of a 50-year-old structure into an architecturally dramatic and stylish entertainment center. The main level incorporates high-tech wall, floor, ceiling and lighting materials including multi-colored wall-tiles, pendant and neon lighting, and a new flooring material designed specifically for heavy traffic area. Architectural details include space-coffered ceilings, a canopied entranceway, brass railings and marble pari-mutuel counters. The

grandstand food court, designed in bright, energetic colors houses six vendors offering cuisine from grilled burgers to homemade cookies.

The Sports Lounge & Bar, in the upper clubhouse, is filled with mauves, pinks, grays and dark blues set against natural oak woodwork and neon accents. The plush lounge and bar is surrounded by big-screens simulcasting all major sporting events as well as airing live coverage and replays of the greyhound races.

The Clubhouse Dining Room offers an upscale atmos-phere for more formal dining. Architectural details include a marble entranceway, vaulted

ceiling, art deco chandelier and a dramatic full-length wall mirror that serves as a back-drop. Mahogany woodwork and a sophisticated palette of colors including mauve, gray, and burgundy complete the look of this elegant dining room that seats 300.

The total renovation, during which not a single day's receipts were lost, means that patrons can now enjoy grey-hound racing in a casino-like atmosphere that is both stylish and exciting.

The Wakaya Club
Wakaya Island, Fiji

PROJECT TYPE:
Island Beach Resort

DESIGN TEAM:
David and Jill Gilmour, Adrian Sofield

ARCHITECTURAL/DESIGN FIRM:
Tubukolo Builders

PROJECT SIZE:
Eight 2-guest cottages

PHOTOGRAPHY:
© Larry Dale Gordon

In the Wakaya Club, the integrity of Fijian construction has been elevated to an international standard of luxury targeting the most sophisticated of international travelers. Wakaya, a privately owned five-square-mile island in the Fijian archipelago is ringed by coral reefs and almost three dozen shell-strewn beaches. The club's 200 acres face a stunning 1.5 mile beach at the northwest edge of the island, and its eight sunset-facing bures or cottages provide accommodations for only sixteen guests.

The cottages, shaded by coconut palms and featuring outdoor verandas, each provide 1,500 square feet of indoor space. The tropical climate is tempered by banks of cross-ventilating windows and fans hung from the high-beamed cathedral ceilings. Wide manicured lawns and gardens filled with lush tropical flora ensure maximum privacy for each couple. Palm Grove is the central bure, and has a 65-foot-high ceiling constructed entirely of giant timbers covered with layers of thatch. It serves as the dining

area, where four talented chefs provide both Fijian and international cuisine.

Outdoor leisure facilities include the synthetic grass tennis court, the international standard croquet lawn, and the nine-hole golf course that winds its way through the island's innumerable palm trees. The resort also provides deep-sea fishing charters, scuba diving expeditions, windsurfing, sailing and sight-seeing trips. All activities are provided free of charge and only top professional equipment is provided.

II
PART

Spas

Titan Fitness Center
Stamford, Connecticut

Brenner's Spa
Baden-Baden, Germany

Norwich Spa
Norwich, Connecticut

The Naniloa Hotel Spa
Hilo, Hawaii

Canyon Ranch in the Berkshires
Lenox, Massachusetts

Doral Saturnia Spa
Miami, Florida

The Spa at the Peninsula Hotel
New York, New York

Equinox Fitness Center
New York, New York

Grand Hyatt Wailwea
Maui, Hawaii

■

Titan Fitness Center
Stamford, Connecticut

PROJECT TYPE:
Health/Exercise Facility

DESIGN TEAM:
Julia F. Monk, AIA, ASID, Partner-in-charge; William Whistler, Design Director; Christina Hauer, Project Designer; Rafael Banzil, Project Architect

ARCHITECTURAL/DESIGN FIRM:
Brennan Beer Gorman Monk/Interiors

PROJECT SIZE:
8,000 square feet

BUDGET:
$600,000

PHOTOGRAPHY:
© Peter Paige

Comprising the second floor of the World Wrestling Federation's four-story office complex in Stamford, Connecticut, this health center was designed to fulfill a variety of needs. Most important-ly, it is the central training center for the Federation's professional wrestlers, body builders, athletes, and trainers. Therefore, it requires the latest in state-of-the-art fitness equipment. The flooring in the weight-training and aero-bics areas is cushioned to pro-vide impact reduction, and is covered with special anti-fungal carpeting.

Since the club is also used by the federation's employees and public members, the area had to retain a non-threatening look that appeals to the aver-age user while presenting a theatrical, studio-like atmos-phere suitable for televised promotional spots. The facili-ty's physical layout and mas-sive structural columns are accented with bold primary colors with brash neon lighting and signage. Zebra uphol-stered seating assists in creat-ing a space as flashy and bois-terous as the sport of profes-sional wrestling itself. High ceilings, wrap-around floor-to-ceiling windows and mirrored walls give the space an extremely open appearance.

PART

Brenner's Spa
Baden-Baden, Germany

PROJECT TYPE:
Spa

DESIGN TEAM:
Countess Douglas

ARCHITECTURAL/DESIGN FIRM:
Professor Casar Pinau; Michael von Heppe

PHOTOGRAPHY:
Courtesy of Mari Homi Int'l Public Relations

The Brenner's Spa is a composite of a charming Grand Hotel in the finest Old World tradition with the modern facilities of a private clinic. Shades of washed green and yellow combine with mixed browns and creams to create an allusion of summer breezes wafting through the spa. A deep green tiled spa adds richness and intensity while highlighting the dark foliage. A scene of Roman women visiting a spa adds a touch of intimacy and detail to this simple, soothing environment.

Roman details grace the walls in the Pool area as well, with Doric columns dramatically marking the full windowscape at one end of the pool. Coral walls, soft green lighting, and the blue tiled pool combine to create a brilliant color scheme which complements the greenery visible through the window. During the colder months, cool white lighting replaces the warm green of the summer months, creating an experience best described as swimming in a Winter Wonderland. The upholstery on the lounging chairs changes with the seasons also. By synchronizing the pool with the windowscape, the designers have enveloped the natural environment into their design scheme, giving this indoor pool an outdoor feeling.

Norwich Spa
Norwich, Connecticut

PROJECT TYPE:
Spa/ Beauty Treatment

DESIGN TEAM:
Charles P. Swerz, Principal; H. Spence Sutton, Associate

DESIGN FIRM:
Charles P. Swerz, Interior Design

PAINTED FINISHES AND MURALS:
Patrick Kennedy, Kennedy/Page Associates

PROJECT SIZE:
14,000 square feet

BUDGET:
$1.4 million

PHOTOGRAPHY:
© Peter Paige

Allusions to past glories abound at the Spa at Norwich Inn, a luxury facility whose formal layout reflects the balance and symmetry of the classical era. The focal point of the spa, the pool room, lies beyond the lobby and serves as the cross-axis of visual activity. A muted polychrome palette is used throughout the facility, and custom plaster wall sconces bathe the twenty-three foot vaulted ceilings with light. The pool is decorated in an elaborate mosaic of cobalt blue, gold, and white. Guests at the spa can gaze out at the New England countryside through an eighteen foot tall Palladian window. On either side of the pool room are the aerobics room and the gym featuring state of the art Kaiser Cam II, Universal, Trotter Treadmill, Stairmaster, and Liferower equipment. In addition, there are separate bath houses for both men and women featuring sauna, steam, and whirlpool facilities. The spa also offers eight private massage rooms, loofa, hydrotherapy, herbal wrap, and beauty treatment rooms. A thoroughly modern facility designed to accommodate expansion as needed, the Spa at Norwich Inn will continue to be state of the art well into the twenty-first century.

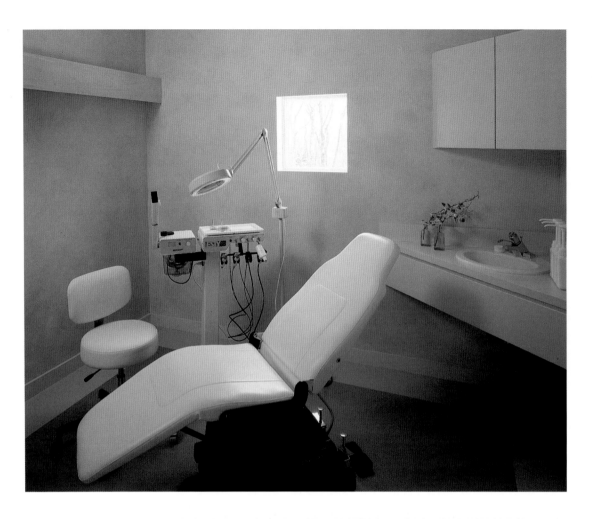

The Naniloa Spa
Hilo, Hawaii

PROJECT TYPE:
Hotel Spa

DESIGN TEAM:
Michael James Leineweber, AIA, Vice Chairman
(Project Director); R. Ted Matheny, Project
Manager; Donna Yuen, AIA, Architectural
Designer; Lauren Bosel, Interior Designer; Mark
Farineau, Construction Contract Administrator

ARCHITECTURAL/DESIGN FIRM:
Media Five Limited

PROJECT SIZE:
6,000 square feet

BUDGET:
$1,043,428

PHOTOGRAPHY:
© Ron Starr

This 5,200 square foot spa, on the ground and first floor levels of the hotel, is accessible through the hotel's main lobby. The arcade serves as the spa's spine to organize traffic flow, with sconce lighting showcasing the colonnade and its vaulted ceiling, complemented by a flooring of ceramic tile with marble insets of muted earth tones. The aerobics room is the spa's single largest space with 850 square feet. Sited to overlook Hilo Bay, the room is glassed on three sides with a mirror on the fourth. A vaulted ceiling of wooden slats and indirect lighting increases the room's sense of spaciousness; pairs of double doors open to a grassy lawn area bordering the bay. The spa contains a unisex sauna and steam room, and men's and women's locker rooms visually linked with four colors in a spectrum from blue to pale mauve.

A raised and tiled floor creates the entrance to the hot tub and cold plunge area, that features marble accent walls and a decorative, shell-shaped fountain. The gym offers free weights and exercise machines, including treadmills and bicycles, and carpeted flooring for added comfort. Bifold doors line one wall, opening the room to the swimming pool deck.

The aesthetics salon, located on the upper level, offers facials and skin treatments in four private rooms. Each area has its own climate and music controls to increase the sense of privacy; carpeting, marble counters and rattan furniture in warm earth tones contribute to the atmosphere of elegant relaxation.

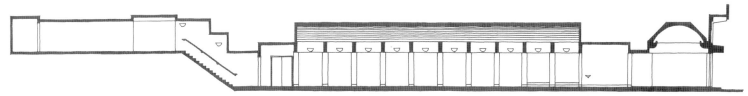

LONGITUDINAL SECTION

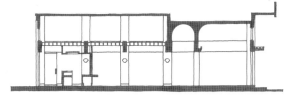

TRANSVERSE SECTION

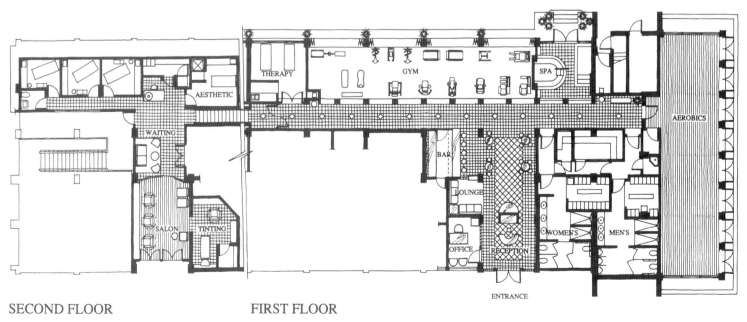

SECOND FLOOR   FIRST FLOOR

Canyon Ranch in the Berkshires
Lenox, Massachusetts

PROJECT TYPE:
New England Health Resort

DESIGN TEAM:
Bruce Johnson, Lead Architect

ARCHITECTURAL/DESIGN FIRM:
Jung Bannen Associates

PROJECT SIZE:
120 rooms, 100,000 square foot spa

PHOTOGRAPHY:
Courtesy of Canyon Ranch, Inc.

Canyon Ranch in the Berkshires is the only major co-ed health and fitness vacation resort open year-round in the northeastern United States, and is located on 120 acres of woodlands in Lenox, Massachusetts. The architectural focal point of the ranch, the historic marble and brick Bellefontaine mansion, was built in 1897 by the architects who designed the New York Public Library for the Astors, and is a copy of Louis XVI's Petit Trianon. The mansion's fully-restored interior contains the original historic library

wing with its wood and marble trimmed fireplace and 10-foot-high bookshelves, gracious dining rooms, and the medical, behavioral health, and movement therapy departments.

Ranch activities center around the cutting-edge, 100,000-square-foot, three-level spa. The spa features exercise and weight training rooms; indoor tennis, racquet-ball and squash courts; indoor swimming pool and jogging track; herbal and massage rooms; and skin care and beauty salons. Men's and women's spa facilities include

saunas, steam rooms, whirlpool baths, lockers and showers. While at the ranch, guests stay in a modern two-story inn, offering 120 comfortable guest rooms and luxury suites. The mansion, spa and inn are connected by all-weather, glass-enclosed walkways and surround a historic reflecting pool and formal garden. Additional outdoor facilities at the ranch include a 50-foot swimming pool, tennis and platform courts, and miles of trails for walking, hiking, biking and cross-country skiing.

Doral Saturnia Spa
Miami, Florida

PROJECT TYPE:
Health Spa

DESIGN TEAM:
Jung Brannen Associates

ARCHITECTURAL/DESIGN FIRM:
Jung Brannen Associates; Tom Lee Limited

PROJECT SIZE:
48 suites, 3 buildings

PHOTOGRAPHY:
© Dan Forer, Dan Forer Photography

Inspired by the Italian spa Terme de Saturnia, this American luxury spa merges ancient Roman hedonism, Renaissance palaces and Palladian villas to stunning, elegant effect. A superb complement to the adjacent Doral Country Club, the spa comprises three buildings with walls of locally mined Tuffa stone and terra cotta roofing that encircle a large central garden.

There is a stunning, three-story art nouveau double stairway of Bronze fountains designed by artist Emilio-Jacques Ruhlmann for the Paris department store Bon Marché. The chiseled glass panels are by Dennis Abbe, while the Boticelli-inspired mural panels were painted by Washington D.C. artist Brad Stevens. Abundant greenery and floral touches personalize the space while serving to blend the interior environ-

ment with the wonderful garden that it surrounds.

There are 48 guest suites, and the 5-star spa facilities include both indoor and outdoor pools, a dozen massage rooms, exercise rooms, mud baths, private sun bathing areas, water therapy and recreation rooms for dancing and aerobics. Among other amenities the spa offers are a professional hair salon and three restaurants.

The Spa at the Peninsula Hotel
New York, New York

PROJECT TYPE:
Hotel Spa

ARCHITECTURAL/DESIGN FIRM:
Pilat-Davis Architects

PROJECT SIZE:
242 guest rooms

BUDGET:
$127 million (price of hotel)

PHOTOGRAPHY:
Property of Peninsula New York

The historic Gotham Hotel, on New York's Fifth Avenue, was transformed in 1988 into the Peninsula Hotel, a landmark hotel in the style of the Belle Epoque period. The charm of this gracious hotel is derived largely from the Art Nouveau furnishings that grace the hotel's interiors, including a sofa, bergere chairs, and gallery tables by the Art Nouveau master Louis Majorelle. Entering into the lobby is like stepping directly into the Belle Epoque, an era noted for its grandeur and elegance. The grand sweeping staircase that leads to the hotel's restaurants, mezzanine, and reception area is constructed of rich Biance Classico marble imported from Italy. Artists painstakingly

painted a similar faux marble pattern on the old Gotham's corinthian columns to achieve the rich feeling of marble throughout. Dominating center stage on the staircase landing is a magnificent original Art Nouveau armoire by French designer J. Cherbonnier. The majestic multi-faceted crystal chandelier imported from Europe warmly highlights the ornate Renaissance details of the restored original ceiling.

In addition to the original Art Nouveau pieces, many other pieces are displayed throughout the Hotel, including original photographs by Sarah Bernhardt and original prints by Alphonse Mucha. Designer Howard Hirsch traveled throughout Europe pur-

chasing the antiques featured; pieces he couldn't find were custom designed.

The Peninsula has a tripartite composition and a frontage of five bays on Fifth Avenue with a facade of hand-carved limestone. Its two-story rusticated base features a ground-story arcade and square mezzanine windows. Visually linked with the University Club by the lower cornices and the ninth-story balcony, the restored crowning cornice was painted with a unique plastic paint to simulate the effect of aging. A giant Doric portal flanked by banded columns further harmonizes with the University Club, creating a continuity recognized even while the building was still under construction in 1902.

Equinox Fitness Center
New York, New York

PROJECT TYPE:
Health/Exercise Facility

ARCHITECTURAL/DESIGN FIRM:
Mojo-Stumer Architects

PROJECT SIZE:
15,000 square feet

PHOTOGRAPHY:
© Phillip Ennis

The scale of the lower level fitness area was such that an open, loft-like environment was created allowing for a reading of a reinforced perimeter inside of which various "elements" (volumes) and activities occurred. A strong axiality from the front reception area back toward a focal point space between the men's and ladies' locker rooms extenuates the expansive character of this club. With the addition, the focal point aspect of the original plan was exploited by placing an open interconnecting stair between the locker rooms, continuing the established line of circulation.

While retaining the character of the lower level, a vehicle garage with wide column spacing, the stair builds upon existing conditions while relating to the previous counterpart. Although the scales were much different, the "loft like" feeling of the downstairs was continued in the expansion through the use of discreet elements that bridge/unify both spaces. Despite the lower ceilings of the upstairs, an illusion of a larger scaled space with its own internally generated sight lines and perspectives was achieved, through a unique use of color and materials.

The client was able to maintain a sense of overall continuity while providing an option of differently sized environments in which members could participate in their activities.

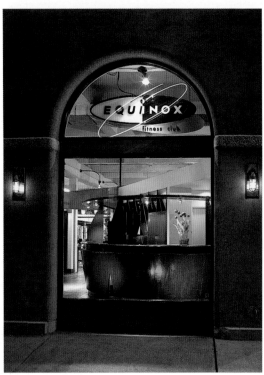

Grand Hyatt Wailea
Maui, Hawaii

PROJECT TYPE:
Spa

DESIGN TEAM:
Robert E. Barry, Designer; Danny Laureano, Project Manager; Bernie Miranda, Project Manager; Charles Lee, Project Coordinator; Alisa Chodos, Project Manager in charge of Decoration

ARCHITECTURAL/DESIGN FIRM:
Barry Design Associates

PROJECT SIZE:
50,000 sq. ft.

BUDGET:
$640 million (hotel)

PHOTOGRAPHY:
© Jaime Ardiles-Arce

This spa, the largest in the United States, has a European character very different from the Hawaiian flavor of the rest of the Hotel. Bathed in a soothing monochromatic color scheme of cream, white, taupe, and beige, the Reception area inspires relaxation even before guests enter the spa. A patterned marble floor delineates specific areas of the reception room while complementing the classical statuary. Gentle lighting is provided by a Lalique chandelier, with bamboos, palms, and other tropical foliage adding a dramatic influx of color and life.

Reminiscent of Roman baths, the wet area utilizes sturdy, easy maintenance material such as glass blocks and terrazzo flooring without

compromising style. Finishes of granite and marble contribute to the classical theme, with a Greek key patterned mosaic in the individual compartments. Reiterating the Greek key pattern, the backlit dome establishes continuity, while its greenish hue encompasses the tropical elements of the spa, the palms and foliage, in the classical theme.

Details from the wet area such as the mosaics and tropical foliage are repeated in the tub area, but special touches are added, giving this space a unique feeling without abandoning the theme and continuity of the spa. A large dome harkens to Roman architectural elements, while the gallery on the second floor imitates the Public baths of ancient

Rome. The wrought iron details have an antique feel while soft touches of brass give the room glitter and warmth. Secluded seating beneath a tetrastyle portico decorated with prints of Roman women affords a perfect vantage point, while the crystal wall sconces and the painted garland pattern extenuate the circularity and openness of this space.

The game room, reminiscent of the English Manor Style, sports a coffered ceiling finished in mahogany, Chippendale upholstered chairs, and framed and matted sporting prints. Extensive wood and verdigris marble completes the rich, royal feel of this leisure spot.

III PART

Resorts

Villas Quinta Real
Puerto Vallarta, Mexico

Brays Island Plantation
Sheldon, South Carolina

Pflaum's Posthotel Pegnitz
Pegnitz, Germany

Uwharrie Point Lodge
Denton, North Carolina

Resort at Squaw Creek
Olympic Valley, California

Cheeca Lodge
Islamorada, Florida

The Barton Creek Resort
Austin, Texas

Hôtel du Palais
Biarritz, France

The Phoenician
Scottsdale, Arizona

The Maui Prince Hotel
Kihei, Hawaii

Hyatt Coral Grand
Puerto Vallarta, Mexico

Forte Hotel Village
Cagliari, Italy

Halekulani
Honolulu, Hawaii

Santiburi Dusit Resort
Koh Samui, Thailand

Carnival Cruises
Fantasy

Celebrity Cruises
The Zenith

■

Villas Quinta Real
Puerto Vallarta, Mexico

PROJECT TYPE:
Resort Hotel

DESIGN TEAM:
Arq. Roberto Elias Pessah and Arq. Ricardo Elias
Pessah, Directors of Architecture & Interior Design

ARCHITECTURAL/DESIGN FIRM:
ELIAS + ELIAS ARQUITECTOS

PROJECT SIZE:
50 suites and 25 villas

BUDGET:
$16 million

PHOTOGRAPHY:
© Alejandro López Ramirez/Professional
Photographer

A tropical mansion filled with the highest quality Mexican furnishings and details, the Villas Quinta Real is a landmark building located in the center of Marina Vallarta's private championship golf course.

Original fixed pieces by Mexican artist Sergio Bustamente are complemented by special hand-crafted and painted furniture from the artisan village Michoacan, with each piece being different and unique. For example, sculpted masks and fish inhabit one bedroom, while a triptych of foliage and water occupies another. The floors are tiled in cool earthy tones of coral, gray and blue, and arched details on walls and doorways create a feeling of depth and circulation. Nine junior suites offer balconies and full marble baths with brass fittings; twenty master suites have private terrace pools overlooking the 18th fairway, while twelve Grand Class suites contain jacuzzis overlooking the golf course and tropical pond.

Contrasting with the cool, subtle hues of the rooms, the Lobby adds rich greens, blues and raspberry, with set stones bordering the coral tiling. Even the dining room, encircled by large arched doors remains unique without violating the theme of the hotel.

PART III

Brays Island Plantation
Sheldon, South Carolina

PROJECT TYPE:
Real Estate Development

DESIGN TEAM:
R. Christian Schmitt, AIA, ASID; Thorndyke
Williams

ARCHITECTUAL DESIGN FIRM:
Chris Schmitt & Associates, Inc.; Thorndyke
Williams Interior Design

PROJECT SIZE:
Plantation & out buildings

BUDGET:
$1.5 million

PHOTOGRAPHY:
© Rion Rizzo, Creative Sources Photography

The Brays Island Plantation is a project that preserved a 5,000 acre plantation by developing it in a very unique and sensitive manner. A 325-acre block of the plantation is divided into one-acre homesites, while the balance of the land is owned in common. Emphasis is placed upon stewardship of the land, which is managed as a hunting and shooting preserve with a small portion set aside for a private golf course and other recreational facilities.

The existing plantation house and its adjacent carriage house were transformed into a 15-suite inn with club facilities. The inside and outside of the building are entirely renovated, as is the indoor swimming pool which dated to the 1960s. Additions to the complex included a storage shed and service areas, wood trellises to screen the indoor pool structure,, a new outdoor swimming pool, and two clay tennis courts. The existing farm buildings were renovat-

ed, and now serve as an equestrian center and a real estate sales office. These various utilitarian buildings were tied together through the development of a central area with riding ring, carefully detailed custom fencing and other landscape elements. Overalll the project succeeds in creating a comfortable, first class facility that looks as of it has been part of the plantation and its beautiful natural setting for a very long time.

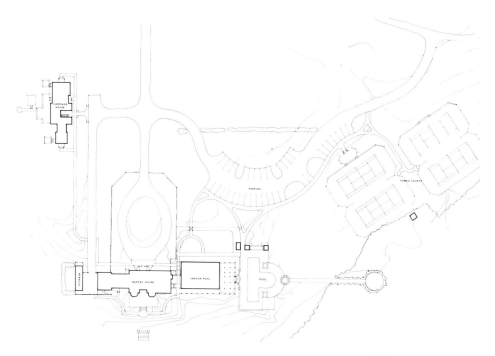

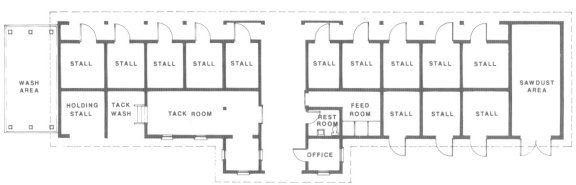

EQUESTRIAN CENTER

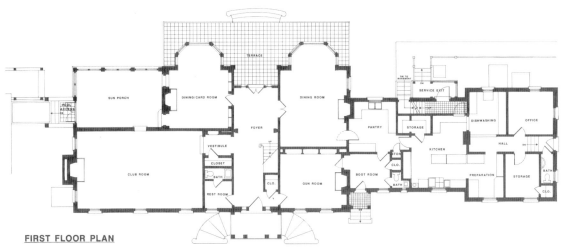

FIRST FLOOR PLAN

SECOND FLOOR PLAN

CARRIAGE HOUSE FIRST FLOOR PLAN

CARRIAGE HOUSE SECTION

Pflaum's Posthotel Pegnitz
Pegnitz, Germany

PROJECT TYPE:
Hotel Suite

DESIGN TEAM:
Dirk Obliers, President; Marianne Obliers, Management; Ralf Kühnast, Designer; Uwe Sinnig, Designer

ARCHITECTURAL/DESIGN FIRM:
Dirk Obliers Design

PROJECT SIZE:
50 guest rooms, 25 suites

PHOTOGRAPHY:
© Dirk Obliers

The result of a fruitful cooperation between visionary, courageous hoteliers and designers keen to experiment, the "Parsifal suite" is comparable with the Grand Hotel and the splendor of the Belle Epoque at the beginning of the 20th century. Living and sleeping in this one-of-a-kind suite allows guests to forget the daily work routine and refresh their senses—it is an incomparable plunge into another world. The sleeping cave is a room-in-a-room design, constructed in metal, mirrors, and cutting-edge fiber optics. The bathroom also utilizes a similarly unusual material combination: colored slate and perforated plate-metal. Carpet and seating also designed by Dirk Obliers round out the design.

The recently completed indoor golf course 'Orpheus Plays Golf' gives the impression of a new and unusual spaciousness. This new addition to the hotel's existing fitness and whirlpool centers is another captivating design that reflects a blend of extraordinary ideas, formal language and innovative material combinations. The interplay between the glittering stone carpet, bubbling water walls and heads, the stainless steel walls indirectly lit by blue lights, the arched stainless steel footbridge, the ceiling-high sandstone bodies and adjoining light tunnel offers new adventures in the game of golf. Peepshows in the stainless steel walls provide information about the hotel and outdoor golfing.

While descending into the secrets of the underworld, one experiences 2000 sparkling light spots in the "Black Grotto" - the jacuzzi. Colorful Kaolin, (layers of earth from the surrounding area and glittering granite), stone carpet and bubbling walls of water form the fascinating setting for the steam bath, sauna, rest area and massage room.

The hackneyed reproduction of a Mediterranean holiday dream background was avoided in favor of integrating the regional landscape into the design. The end result is a hotel environment -modernly interpreted and designed.

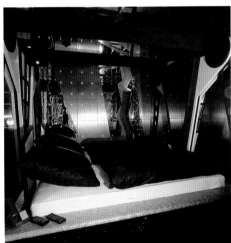

Uwharrie Point Lodge
Denton, North Carolina

PROJECT TYPE:
Visiting lodge for prospective homeowners

DESIGN TEAM:
Cyndi F. Folds, Co-owner and Executive Vice President;
Anne S Bowers, Vice President; Roger D. Ward, Senior
Designer

ARCHITECTURAL/DESIGN FIRM:
Small Kane Architects; One Design Center, Inc.

PROJECT SIZE:
8 guest rooms

BUDGET:
First phase in $100,000,000 residential development

PHOTOGRAPHY:
© Carl G. Saporiti

This eight-room guest lodge is located in the heart of a private championship golf course overlooking a 5300-acre lake; but, it is the natural beauty of the adjoining Uwharrie National Forest that sets the theme for this lake-front resort. Entrants to the lodge go through a foyer into a two-story living area with an overhanging balcony. An impressive stone fireplace dominates the interior, while an eclectic mix of Victorian, Shaker, and American furnishings, non-traditional fabrics, and local crafts create a relaxing atmosphere. The main living area is flanked on the right by a small dining room and on the left by a game room, complete with pool table, bar, books, and games. The entire back wall is windowed, focusing on the lakefront, and a long back porch accommodates rocking chairs and Adirondack chairs for "just sitting," and wrought iron furniture for outdoor dining.

Guest rooms are individualized by art and accessories, and appropriately named so that guests can request their favorite. Each room has a balcony overlooking the lake, and indirect lighting, fireplaces, desks and comfortable seating make the guests feel at home.

The Resort at Squaw Creek
Olympic Valley, California

PROJECT TYPE:
Ski Lodge and Resort

DESIGN TEAM:
Phyllis Martin-Vegue, Design Principal; Lamberto Moris, Managing Principal; Carol Padham, Project Manager, Ron Aguila, Project Designer

ARCHITECTURAL/DESIGN FIRM:
Simon Martin-Vegue Winkelstein Moris

PROJECT SIZE:
500,000 square feet, 404 guest rooms

BUDGET:
$6.5 million

PHOTOGRAPHY:
© Chas McGrath

The contextual design of the Resort at Squaw Creek creates a wonderful look of rough-hewn elegance. Site-specific materials and colors fill the project, and were utilized in every phase of its design. For example, boulders excavated from the location were bulldozed into the lobby and are now an intrinsic part of its look. The walls of the Cascade Restaurant are punctuated with Sierra granite pilasters framing rough, stone panels. Flamed and polished granite is used in the lobby flooring, occasional tables, and the rough-finished columns some of which also feature polished stone insets in their center vertical reveals. The lavender palette found in the Glissandi Restaurant is derived from wild flowers found on the site, and the carpet, by Phyllis Martin-Vegue, is based on Native American patterns.

The powerful volume of the public spaces in the resort is enhanced by enormous windows that flood the room with vast quantitues of daylight and offer expansive mountain views. The guest rooms, each with custom-designed furniture and carpeting also have oversized windows to emphasize the site's natural beauty.

Winter sports revolve around the skiing at Squaw Valley, and in the summer, guests revel in the Robert Trent Jones-designed golf course, the outdoor tennis courts and the many hiking and horseback riding trails. For more relaxed pleasures, the resort offers three pools, hot tubs and a full service spa.

Cheeca Lodge
Islamorada, Florida

PROJECT TYPE:
Resort Hotel

DESIGN TEAM:
Phyllis Martin-Vegue, Principal-in-charge; Lamberto Moris, Design Principal; Carol Padham, Project Designer; Doug Tom, Project Architect

ARCHITECTURAL/DESIGN FIRM:
Simon Martin-Vegue Winkelstein Moris

PROJECT SIZE:
203 rooms

BUDGET:
$2 million

PHOTOGRAPHY:
Mark Darley/© Esto Photo Graphics

This site's delightful climate and separation from the mainland give Cheeca a slow-paced, easy going charm. The original design of the lodge was casual and eclectic in response to its relaxed surroundings; renovations tripled the lodge's capacity and added luxury without sacrificing the familiar, clubby, and funky atmosphere of the old Cheeca Lodge. Memorabilia from Cheeca's fishing and golf history, including the reuse of the original pecky cypress panel-ing in the new beamed ceilings and the restoration and reuse of a large collection of old fiberglass fish trophies adds immeasurably to the nostalgic ambiance.

Keystone flooring and columns, custom designed millwork, and brilliant splashes of color added by both the artwork and the profusion of colorful indoor plants are reflective of the surrounding area and create a fresh, informal atmosphere. All fabrics, finishes and materials used are extremely durable, in order to withstand the sea air climate and the terrific abuse of sand and sun. Yet, they are still smooth and pleasant to the touch. Residential scale lighting fixtures including delicate picture lights and large, hand-blown hurricane lamps combine to create dramatic evening moods for this prestigious island fishing retreat.

Barton Creek Resort
Austin, Texas

PROJECT TYPE:
Golf Resort

ARCHITECTURAL/DESIGN FIRM:
Frank Welch & Assoc., Building Designer; HKS, Architects; Gensler & Associates, Interior Design

PROJECT SIZE:
147 guestrooms, 17 executive meeting rooms, 3 buildings

PHOTOGRAPHY:
Courtesy of Barton Creek Resort

Among the most prestigious Golf resorts in the country, Austin's Barton Creek Resort features three eighteen-hole championship golf courses designed by Tom Fazio, Arnold Palmer and Ben Crenshaw. The resort was designed to serve as a private country club as well as a center for corporate and executive meetings. The resort, which follows a handcrafted, environmentally-balanced theme, blends effortlessly with the surrounding Hill Country landscape, and was constructed without harming nearby Barton Creek, the natural habitat of threatened native bird species.

The resort features a European-style spa, health and fitness center that offers an indoor pool and jogging track, par course, weight training equipment, rigorous wellness programs, and private health studios for men and women with sauna, steam bath and hydrotherapy. The wide range of personal services that are available include massage, facials, loofah body rubs, and herbal wrap treatments. Eight distinctive restaurants, ranging from the formal Palm Court to the relaxed and casual Grille serve the club. Additional recreational facilities for club members include twelve hard surface tennis courts, volleyball courts, a billiards room, horseback riding and water sports at nearby Lake Travis.

Hôtel du Palais
Biarritz, France

PROJECT TYPE:
Luxury Beach Hotel

DESIGN TEAM:
Edouard Jean Niermans, Architect

PROJECT SIZE:
139 guest rooms, 21 suites

PHOTOGRAPHY:
Courtesy of Hôtel du Palais

Originally built as a summer palace for Napoleon III in 1854, the Palace became a Hotel in 1880 after the end of the Empire. Destroyed in 1903 by fire, and rebuilt in 1905 with an added wing, the Hôtel du Palais is an historical landmark that delights the traveler of today as it has for almost a century and a half. Although centered on the stunning Biarritz beach, the hotel is within a hundred yards of the city center and close to the casino.

The Hôtel du Palais offers three restaurants: "La Rotonde" a grand banquet room facing the Atlantic Ocean, "Le Grand Siècle" for quiet dinners, and "L'Hippocampe" for poolside lunches. Two bars are also featured: Le Bar Impérial, and the swimming pool bar. The heated, seawater swimming pool offers direct access to the beach. Ocean-oriented activities include beach diving, surfing and windsurfing. Health facilities at the hotel include a solarium, fitness club and sauna. There is an on-site golf pitching green, and eight eighteen-hole golf courses nearby, as well as tennis courts, horseback riding and bullfights.

A living testimony to the history of Biarritz, France and Europe, the Hôtel du Palais has been a hotel, casino, hospital for the wounded of World War I, and a showplace for the style of the roaring '20s. Now, however, it has been restored to its original splendor, appropriately accommodating today's rich and famous.

The Phoenician
Scottsdale, Arizona

PROJECT TYPE:
Resort Hotel

ARCHITECTURAL/DESIGN FIRM:
Killingsworth, Stricker, Lindgren, Wilson &
Associates; Dwayne Lewis

PROJECT SIZE:
60,000 suite, 580 Rooms

PHOTOGRAPHY:
Courtesy of The Phoenician

Designed to attract the high-end leisure traveler as well as the high-end corporate meeting and incentive market, the Phoenician sprawls magnificently in a 130-acre desert setting at the base of Camelback mountain. A totally unique architectural approach was taken with the Phoenician, with all construction based on radians and degrees rather than right angles or straight lines. The Main structure, one-quarter mile long and containing over 84,000+ cubic yards of "cast in place" concrete, is crescent-shaped, and steps back at the

front and ends so that no two rooms or corridors are stacked one directly above the other.

The resort's centerpiece is its championship eighteen-hole golf course, which hosts national events and includes a driving range, putting green, pro shop and men's and women's locker rooms. The Tennis Garden features eleven lighted tennis courts, two employing the new "Rebound Ace" surface from Australia, one a dedicated practice court with ball machine, and one a center court with full spectator seating. Men's and women's

locker rooms and full instruction are also available. A total of seven pools are here, including an oval pool lined in mother-of-pearl tiles, an exotic whirlpool, and a children's pool with a 165-foot water slide. Other outdoor features include the tournament croquet lawn, a sand volleyball court, lawn bowling (bocce), walking/jogging/hiking trails, and a cactus garden containing 350 varieties of cacti and succulents comprising the northern two acres of the site.

Maui Prince Hotel at Wakena Resort
Kihei, Hawaii

PROJECT TYPE:
Beach Resort

DESIGN TEAM:
Riki Wantanabe of Q-Designees

ARCHITECTURAL/DESIGN FIRM:
Anbe, Aruga & Ishizu Architects Inc.

PROJECT SIZE:
310 guest rooms

PHOTOGRAPHY:
Courtesy of Maui Prince Hotel

The only hotel located on 1800 acres of secluded beaches, the Maui Prince Hotel offers its guests an intimate place to retreat and relax while enjoying the magnificent vistas of the ocean and mountains. Cascading waterfalls designed by Hideyuki Shibata and a 320,000 gallon Koi Fish Mirror Pond enhance the natural beauty rather than dominate it.

Rooms portray the easy tropical lifestyle, and are deco-rated simply so as not to detract from the marvelous window views. Mono-chromatic coloring, an abundance circulation of light and air create a cool environment, highlighted by subtle tropical patterns, floral arrangements, and traditional Koawood furniture.

In designing the hotel's two eighteen-hole golf courses, Robert Trent Jones, Jr. also preserved the natural beauty of the site, adapting the cours-es to the existing terrain. Recognized as one of the most challenging and spectacular courses in the state, the combination of harmony with challenge has created on atmosphere reminiscent of a Zen Garden. The course, formerly the site of the EPSON PGA Senior Stats Match broadcast by ESPN, was rated one of Hawaii's ten best by *Golf Digest* magazine.

Hyatt Coral Grand
Puerto Vallarta, Mexico

PROJECT TYPE:
Resort Hotel

DESIGN TEAM:
Felipe Valdes Mar; Samuel Moreno Iturbide

ARCHITECTURAL/DESIGN FIRM:
Grupo Top, S.A. de C.V.

PROJECT SIZE:
120 rooms

PHOTOGRAPHY:
© John G. Youden; © Sergio Toledano

The Hyatt Coral Grand in Puerto Vallarta is an exclusive "Boutique Resort," located on the edge of the Sierra Madre mountain range on its own secluded beach. Surrounded by sheltering gardens and waterfalls, the Hotel's luxurious pool offers a shallow area for sunbathing, and a bar where you can be served without ever having to leave the waterfalls. An illuminated tennis court, full spa, and facilities for practicing golf before playing at one of several nearby golf courses are sure to satisfy the sports enthusiast.

Offering breathtaking views, Club Chee Chee is a complex of terraced dining areas built into a hillside above Banderas Bay that accommodates up to 600 people on its multi-levels without sacrificing the privacy and individuality characteristic of this resort. The owner's private villa is available for parties up to sixty people, offering smaller groups special resort accommodations typically available only to large groups. Located on its own jetty, the villa can be reached by road, or via catamarans, with a stop-off for snorkeling or sunning.

Each of the 120 rooms have their own sitting area, private balcony, and oceanfront view. Tiled floors and patterned bedspreads reflect the Mexican heritage, while a wide expanse of doors and windows extenuates the flow of light that characterizes this open air hotel. Minimal furniture coupled with hanging baskets, palms, fruit trays and floral arrangements merges the rooms with the natural beauty of the site, creating an allusion of being outside while enjoying all of the comforts the rooms have to offer.

Forte Hotel Village
Cagliari, Italy

PROJECT TYPE:
Resort Hotel

DESIGN TEAM:
Eric Blakemore; Luciano Deplano

PROJECT SIZE:
433 Bungalows

PHOTOGRAPHY:
© Mauro Galligani

A Mediterranean-style holiday resort in a pinewood setting, the Forte Hotel village is a relaxed and easygoing beach hotel filled with the best of leisure activities. The village has seventeen tennis courts on site, as well as a football pitch, volleyball and squash courts and a fully equipped health club. Ocean-related activities including windsurfing and sailing, diving, and simply lounging by the beach are trademarks of this resort. The five pools are split-level, enhanced by a waterfall and slides. Due to the temperate climate, many terraces were designed into the project to allow for open-air dining. The hotel grounds are teeming with plants, trees and flowers that add a great amount of natural beauty to the site.

Flooded in tans and soft browns, the rooms balance the landscape and foliage. Walls resembling knotty pine complemented by simple floral prints create a peaceful, soothing interior environment, punctuated with palms and other tropical foliage. The Hotel's spa continues the terra cotta theme, with a patterned flooring of reddish-brown tiles.

Halekulani
Honolulu, Hawaii

PROJECT TYPE:
Beach Resort

ARCHITECTURAL/DESIGN FIRM:
Killingsworth, Stricken, Lendgren, Wilson and Associates

PROJECT SIZE:
456 guest rooms

PHOTOGRAPHY:
© David Franzen Photography

Filled with tranquil courtyards and gardens overlooking the ocean, the new Halekulani reflects a simple, serene, and understated elegance rarely found in modern Honolulu. In order to link the grace and elegance of its past with a modern, updated design, the Halekulani hotel incorporated the original 1930s building into a new design consisting of five interconnected buildings ranging from two to sixteen stories. The "old" Main Building had a distinctive style characterized by a high pitched hip roof, reminiscent of the South Pacific. Designed to catch the cooling trade winds, the Dickey roof, named after C.W. Dickey the architect, is repeated as a motif throughout the new building design.

Due to its location in the heart of Waikiki, creating an intimate, garden setting in an urban area became an architectural and design challenge that was achieved in part by the use of a fountain and waterfalls at the busy Waikiki entrance to mask traffic noise and other disruptions from the street paths. Also, more than half of the site's acreage is dedicated to open space. Two courtyards with garden settings enhance the hotel's theme as an "oasis of tranquility in the heart of Waikiki." The resort's finishing touch is the signature Orchid pool, designed after an award-winning Cattleya orchid and created from over 1 1/4 million Italian glass mosaic tiles.

Santiburi Dusit Resort
Koh Samui, Thailand

PROJECT TYPE:
Resort Hotel

DESIGN FIRM:
Leo Design Co., Ltd.

PROJECT SIZE:
77 rooms

PHOTOGRAPHY:
Courtesy of Dusit Hotels & Resorts

With the architecture of the resort modeled after traditional Thai homes, Santiburi Dusit Resort offers a truly Thai experience, harmonizing well with the tranquil Mae Nam Bay setting. Set on a 23-acre site faced by a stunning 300 meter beach, the resort provides guests with the privacy and luxury of 59 individual villas and 16 deluxe Equatorial suites, each with a private veranda. The individual villas have the feel of a traditional Thai home with their wooden floors and Siamese-style art; they are further enhanced by luxuriously designed bathrooms. All units include compact disc stereos, video players, and individual coffee and tea bars. Two suite-style villas each feature a private jacuzzi and tropical garden. The two-story Equatorial Suites each feature a cool sitting room and private balcony downstairs and a large bedroom on the upper floor. Like the Villas, all interior furnishings are of classic Thai design.

Among the extensive recreational and sports facilities offered are a 50 meter swimming pool, two tennis courts, and an extensive health club with squash court, aerobics studio, gym room, sauna, and traditional Thai massage. Water activities such as sailing, windsurfing, yachting and scuba diving are also available. Restaurants include the main dining room, which serves fresh seafood and traditional Royal Thai dishes, and the casual Beach Bar that provides all-day service to those sunning themselves on the sand along the beach or at the pool.

Carnival Cruises "Fantasy"

PROJECT TYPE:
Cruise Ship

DESIGN TEAM:
Joe Farcus

PROJECT SIZE:
2,600 passengers

PHOTOGRAPHY:
© Andy Newman/Carnival Cruise Lines

The Superliner Fantasy incorporates light and color to create an atmosphere aimed at playing on the imagination and senses. Israeli artist Yaacov Agam's 20-foot high kinetic sculpture, a vision of circular motion in gleaming, reflective metal, catches the atrium's changing mood complexions, as well as the attention of the boarding passengers. Other art featured aboard this floating museum of art includes Helen Webber's twelve vast murals created from 5,000 individually sculpted and painted ceramic tiles, as well as over 2,500 oil paintings and original monoprints by abstract impressionist Helen Pierce.

The Grand Spectrum, sort of a shipboard village square, provides entrances to the Fantasy's main centers of activity - the lounges, show-room, pool, and sports deck. Two red-neon-ringed glass elevators provide a spot from which to survey this theater of color which ascends six decks to a huge skylight. The lighting produces rainbow hues absorbed and reflected by the surrounding decor.

Combining art, architecture, and technology, Architect Joe Farcus fashioned an eclectic assembly of environments, from the stylishly intergalactic theme of the Universe Lounge to the more intimate Cleopatra's lined with re-creations of ancient Egyptian mummy cases and artifacts, and covered by a chrome ceiling of pyramid shapes. A Twenty-first Century Bar, Crystal Lounge and Electricity Discotheque are equally distinct and evocative environments created aboard this Fantasy.

Additionally, the Fantasy boasts a 12,000 square foot fitness center in the Nautica Spa. With co-ed whirlpools, 35 modern exercise machines, a wide selection of body and facial treatments, and a 1/8-mile jogging track, the Fantasy offers its passengers ultramodern facilities to stay in shape while getting away from it all.

Celebrity Cruises
The Zenith

PROJECT TYPE:
Cruise Ship

BUILDERS:
Meyer Werft, Germany

INTERIOR DESIGNERS:
A & M Katzourakis; John McNeece

PROJECT SIZE:
1374 passenger capacity

BUDGET:
$210 million

PHOTOGRAPHY:
© Phillip Ennis

The Zenith is dramatic and streamlined in appearance, and features the line's trademark blue and white stack. Constructed in Germany at the Meyer Werft shipyard, the Zenith and her sister ship the Horizon represent the largest passenger ships ever built in the Federal Republic of Germany. Both ships were designed using a CAD system.

Meticulously planned, the Zenith's layout and decor combine superior functionality with comfort, luxury, and aesthetic appeal. Rooms separately maintain a unique and appropriate style without disrupting the design concept carried throughout the entire ship.

The Mayfair Casino recalls the romance and glamour of Monte Carlo, with rich burgundy and navy accented with brass and American cherrywood.

Passengers are offered high energy entertainment in the relaxed setting of the Show Lounge, a theater equipped with state-of-the-art audio/visual equipment and a full-size praecenium stage. Custom carpeting in hues of blue create a festive setting, with added texture and depth provided by elliptical cocktail tables with chrome accent. Additionally, the Showroom contains a dance floor, and can also serve as a meeting room.

Another unique place to spend nights at sea, the Scorpio Discotheque creates an urban, high-tech atmosphere through the use of alternating aqua, pink, and lavender lighting with neon accents, and a mirrored tile ceiling. The centrally-located circular dance floor visually expands the space, while adding to the twenty-first century feel of the disco. Another example of one of the ship's many multi-functional rooms, the Scorpio, operates throughout the daytime as a ship bar, with the high tech lighting system concealed behind a mirrored wall, and the unobtrusively placed disc jockey both.

The Zenith's top deck is home to The Fleet Bar, a crisply Nautical space featuring a panoramic view and a yacht-like atmosphere. Daytime, this room's floor to ceiling windows make the sun and sea a part of the decor. Under the evening sky the Fleet bar, with its piano and dance floor, becomes one of the most inviting settings for a rendez-vous.

Cabins were designed to be as conducive to relaxing as the rest of the ship, featuring large baths, picture windows and oversized closet space. With a continuity of design and attention to passenger comfort, the designers of the Zenith accomplished the seemingly impossible.

Designers' Appendix

A & M Katzourakis
7 Zalokosta street
10671 Athens Greece
Tel. 011.30.1.363.767

Anbe, Aruga & Ishizu Architects, Inc.
1451 South King Road
Honolulu, HI 96814
Tel. (808)949-1025

Barry Design Associates
11601 Wilshire Boulevard
Suite 102
Los Angeles, CA 90025
Tel. (310) 478-6081

Bau Architects & Associates
199-D-3 Uenoya
Naha City, Okinawa Japan

Brennan Beer Gorman Monk / Interiors
515 Madison Avenue
New York, NY 10022
Tel. (212) 888-7667

Charles P. Swerz Interior Design
41 Union Square West
Suite 1121
New York, NY 10003
Tel. (212)627-4222

Chris Schmitt & Associates, Inc.
113 Wappoo Creek Drive
Suite 6
Charleston, SC 29412
Tel. (803) 795-8752

Chris Patillo & Associates
337 17th Street
Oakland, CA 94612

The Dahlin Group Inc.
2671 Crow Canyon Road
San Ramon, CA 94583

dirk obliers design
Friedrich-Ebert-Str. 27
D- 8672 Selb
West Germany
Tel. (09287) 70071

Elias + Elias Arquitectos
Sao Paulo 2393/Providencia
Guadalajara, Jalisco 44620
Mexico
Tel.(3) 641.11.02

EPA
One Fox Grape Road
PO Box 5339
Hilton Head Island, SC 29938

Joe Farcus
c/o Carnival Cruise Lines Corporate Shipbuilding
Koger Center
5225 NW 87th Avenue
Miami, FL 33178

Frank Welch & Associates
703 McKinney
Suite 416
Dallas, TX 75202
Tel. (214)954-0072

Gensler and Associates
900 NCNB Center
700 Louisiana Street
Houston, TX 77002-2728
Tel. (713)228-8050

David & Jill Gilmour
c/o David H. Gilmour & Associates
6525 Sunset Blvd.
Hollywood, CA 90028
Tel. (213)468-9100

Grupo Top, S.A. de C.V.
Insurgetes Sur 1991
Torre "A" Piso 13
Col. San Angel
Mexico, D.F. 01000

Florence "Dottie" Hawkins
Florence Hawkins Interiors
418 Duke Street
Alexandria, VA 22314
Tel. (703)549-8249

Hirsch/Bedner Associates
3216 Nebraska Avenue
Santa Monica, CA 90404
Tel. (310)829-9087

Jos L. Meyer GmbH & Co.
Meyer Werft
Postfach 1120
D-2990 Papenburg 1
West Germany
Tel. 011.49.4961.81.0

Jung/Brannen Associates
177 Milk Street
Boston, MA 02109
Tel. (203)522-2299

Keane Robinson Architects
PO Box 5455
Hilton Head Island, SC 29938

Kennedy/Page Associates
2421 Lake Pancoast Drive
Miami Beach, FL 33140
Tel. (305)534-4060

Killingsworth, Stricker, Lendgren,
Wilson & Associates, Inc.
3833 Long Beach Boulevard
Long Beach, CA 90807

Leo Design Co., Ltd.
7th Floor
Asoke Tower Building 217/16
Sukhumvit 21 Rd.
Bangkok, Thailand

Dwayne Lewis
D.G.L. Architects
3040 North 44th Street
Phoenix, AZ 85028

John McNeece
McNeece Interior Design
2 Holford Yard
Cruikshank Street
London WCIX 9HD England
Tel. 011.44.71.837.1225

Media Five Limited
345 Queen Street
Suite 900
Honolulu, HI 96813
Tel. (808)524-2040

Mojo-Stumer Architects
3 Expressway Plaza
Roslyn Heights, NY 11577
Tel. (516)625-3344

Morris Nathanson Design
163 Exchange Street
Pawtucket, RI 02860
Tel. (401)723-3800

One Design Center, Inc.
2828 Lawndale Drive
PO Box 29426
Greensboro, NC 27429
Tel. (919) 288-03134

Pilat-Davis Architects
95 5th Avenue
New York, NY 10003

Q-Designees
Riki Watanabe
1-13 Yotsuya-Shinjuku-Ku
Tokyo Japan
Tel. 81.3.357.5021

Robert E. Marvin, FASLA
Robert E. Marvin & Associates
Route 4, Box 10
Walterboro, SC 29488
Tel. (803)538-5471

Simon Martin-Vegue Winkelstein Moris
501 Second Street, #701
San Francisco, CA 94107
Tel. (415)546-0400

Small Kane Architects
PO Box 5060
Raleign, NC 27650

Adrian Sofield
PO Box 14465
Suva Fiji
Tel. (679)303-858

Steve Chase Assoc.
70-005 Avenue
PO Box 1610
Rancho Mirage, CA 92270
Tel. (619) 324-4602

Stuart Newman Associates
3191 Coral Way
Suite 204
Miami, FL 33145
Tel. (305) 461-3300

STUDIOS Architecture
99 Green Street
San Fransisco, CA 94111
Tel. (415)398-7575

Thorndyke Williams Interior Design
PO Box 506
Beaufort, SC 29901

Peni Tubukolo
Tubukolo Builders (Fiji) Ltd.
PO Box 57
Deuba Fiji
Tel.(679)450-320

Tom Lee Ltd.
41 East 11th Street
New York, NY 10003
Tel. (212)477-0956

Michael von Heppe
Mittelweg 120
2000 Hamburg 13
Tel. 040-44-71-44

Wimberly Allison Tong & Goo
Kalakaua Avenue
Suite 512
Honolulu, HI 96815 26

Projects' Appendix

Barton Creek Resort
8212 Barton Club Drive
Austin, TX 78735
Tel. (512)329-4000

Brays Island Inn
Brays Island Plantation
Sheldon, SC 29941

Brenner's Spa
Brenner's Park-Hotel
SchillerstraBe 4-6
7570 Baden-Baden

Canyon Ranch In The Berkshires
Bellefontaine, Kemble Street
Lenox, MA 02140
Tel. 1-800-726-9900

Cheeca Lodge
Mile Marker 82
Overseas Highway
Islamorada, FL 33036
Tel. (305)664-4651

Doral Saturnia Spa
8755 Northwest 36th Street
Miami, FL 33178-2401
Tel. (305)593-6030

The Equinox Fitness Center
342 Amsterdam Avenue
New York, NY 10023
Tel. (212)721-4200

The Falls Club
599 Blackhawk Club Drive
Danville, CA 94506

The Fantasy Oceanliner
Carnival Cruises
3655 N.W. 87th Avenue
Miami, FL 33178-2428
Tel. 1-800-327-7373
Tel. 1-800-325-1214(in Florida)

Forte Hotel Village
09010 S. Margherita di Pula
Cagliari, Italy
Tel. 070.92171

Hyatt Coral Grand
PO Box 448
Puerto Vallerta
48300 Jalisco Mexico
Tel. (52.322)2.51.91

Grand Hyatt Wailea
3850 Wailea Alanui Drive
Wailea, HI 96753
Tel. (808)875-1234

Halekulani
2199 Kalia Road
Honolulu, HI 96815-1988
Tel. (808)923-2311

Maui Prince Hotel at Makena Resort
5400 Makena Alanui
Kihei, HI 96753
Tel. (808)874-1111

Mission Bay Gulf Center
1200 6th Street
San Francisco, CA 94107
Tel.(415)431-7888

Hawaii Naniloa Hotel
93 Banyan Drive
Hilo, HI 96720

Norwich Spa
Norwich Inn & Spa
Route 32
Norwich, CT 06360

Hôtel du Palais
1, Avenue de l'Impératrice
64200, Biarritz France
Tel. 33.59.41.64.00

Palm Hills Golf Club House
Okinawa, Japan

The Spa at Peninsula Hotel
The Peninsula New York
700 Fifth Avenue
New York, NY 10019
Tel. (212)247-2200

Pflaum's Posthotel Pegnitz
Nuernberger Str. 14
D- 8570 Pegnitz Germany

The Phoenician
6000 East Camelback Road
Scottsdale, AZ 85251
Tel. (602)423-2405

Santiburi Dusit Resort
12/12 Moo 1 Tambon Mae Nam
Amphur Koh Samui Surat Thani 84140
Thailand
Tel. 077.425.031.38

The South Caroilna Yacht Club
Windmill Harbor Company
PO Box 6133
Hilton Head Island, SC 29938
Tel.(803)842-6050

Resort at Squaw Creek
400 Squaw Creek Road
Olympic Valley, CA 96146
Tel. (916)583-6300

Sunhills Country Club
1000 Yokokura-cho
Utsunomiya-shi
Tochigi Prefecture Japan

Titan Fitness Center
TitanSports Inc.
World Wrestling Federation
Titan Tower
1241 East Main Street
Stamford, CT 06902

Uwharrie Point Lodge
Badin Lake
Denton, NC 27239

Villas Quinta Real
Pelicanos 311 Marina Vallarta
Puerto Vallarta 48300, Mexico
Tel. (91.800)32-732

Wakaya Club
6526 Sunset Boulevard
Hollywood, CA 90028
Tel. (213)468-9100

Wonderland Race Track
190 VFW Parkway
Revere, MA 02151
Tel. (617)284-1300

The Zenith
Celebrity Cruises
950 Third Avenue
New York, NY 10022
Tel. (212)308-6774

Index